AF355538

Unveiling The Silent Mirror

A Repertoire of Poetry

Divyanshu Dixit a.k.a. DD

Copyright © Divyanshu Dixit a.k.a. DD
All Rights Reserved.

This book has been self-published with all reasonable efforts taken to make the material error-free by the author. No part of this book shall be used, reproduced in any manner whatsoever without written permission from the author, except in the case of brief quotations embodied in critical articles and reviews.

The Author of this book is solely responsible and liable for its content including but not limited to the views, representations, descriptions, statements, information, opinions, and references ["Content"]. The Content of this book shall not constitute or be construed or deemed to reflect the opinion or expression of the Publisher or Editor. Neither the Publisher nor Editor endorse or approve the Content of this book or guarantee the reliability, accuracy, or completeness of the Content published herein and do not make any representations or warranties of any kind, express or implied, including but not limited to the implied warranties of merchantability, fitness for a particular purpose.

The Publisher and Editor shall not be liable whatsoever...

Made with ❤ on the BookLeaf Publishing Platform
www.bookleafpub.in
www.bookleafpub.com

Dedication

Dear reader,

I know you struggle to seek yourself in the arcade of life.

This book is for your *too much life*.

I wrote this book for the ones who feel a lot and notices everything.

For the ones who carry a delicate heart and tears and redness in eyes.

For the ones who brainstorms words, actions and behaviors.

I know, it's you and I wrote this book for you!

Just know you are normal and I'm there!

From the first page of validation to the last page of acceptance.

I hope this book gives you a cwtch of love and warmth to be yourself.

~ Live - Love - Laugh ~

With love

Divyanshu Dixit a.k.a. DD <3

Preface

"And you? When will you begin that long journey into yourself?"

~ Rumi

There was a time when I mistook the noise for truth—the constant clamor of roles I had to play, the masks I learned to wear, the mirrors that only ever showed me what the world wanted to see. The noise does not shout, does not demand. It simply exists, waiting patiently to be acknowledged. This book was born in one such moment.

'Unveiling the Silent Mirror' is not a guide, nor a roadmap. It is a companion. A quiet presence beside you as you tread the path inward—toward the unfamiliar, the forgotten, and the often-uncomfortable truths that reside within. This book is not a destination, but a dance— between light and shadow, fear and courage, forgetting and remembering. It is a book written not from a place of having arrived, but from the path itself: broken, beautiful, and ongoing.

These pages are not meant to instruct, but to stir. This book doesn't promise answers. Instead, it offers questions- inviting you to pause, to breathe, to peel back the layers that time, expectation, and fear have carefully placed upon you. If the words resonate with you, it is not because we are the same, but because somewhere, beneath the noise, we are all searching for the same thing: ourselves.

To those standing on the edge of their own silence, unsure of what lies beyond: may this book be a mirror that speaks back, gently and truthfully. This book is for the ones who feel a storm beneath their stillness. The ones who ache without knowing why. The ones who are ready—not to fix themselves, but to finally face themselves.

If you are here, perhaps you too have grown tired of borrowed mirrors.

Come. Let us sit with the silence together.

Divyanshu Dixit a.k.a. DD

Acknowledgements

This book is the result of many quiet hours, countless inner conversations, and the gentle strength of those who held space for me when I could not hold it for myself.
To the silences that didn't break me, but instead taught me how to listen—thank you. You were the beginning.
To my family, whose love has been the quiet constant in my ever-changing world—your presence is the grounding force beneath these words.
To my friends, who saw me in moments when I couldn't see myself, and offered laughter, warmth, and truth—I am endlessly grateful for your light.
To the ones who inspired these pages—through shared stories, chance conversations, and brave vulnerability—you may never know how deeply your reflections shaped mine.
To the readers—thank you for choosing to walk beside me. May you find echoes of your own truth in these pages, and the courage to face your own silent mirror. And lastly, to the self I once abandoned and have since begun to reclaim—this book is for you.

~Divyanshu Dixit a.k.a. DD

1. Silence Matters

From the darkest hours to the brightest days,
I know how bewildered you stand to choose-
Of who you are, or what to say.
I stand to seek the clamour of roles,
From being masked by personalities,
Or the way I hear people for what to do.
I suppose you stand like the pages of books:
Neat and clean with the essence of you.
But you seem more like a cover-
Hideous and mysterious to be known,
Hiding depths from the columns unknown.
I hear the noise that your heart echoes:
The shimmer of innocence,
And the subtle art of ignorance.
Don't be so quiet in the trigger of scenarios.
How ironic your quietness stand
Against the happiness around you.
Your silence matters,
Even if no one hear the noise around you.

2. The Broken Beauty

You are the cradle of being best,
From the havocs of life
To the best of the days.
I know you stand like a moon ablaze,
But it's fine to fall off some days-
Days that feel heavy on heart,
Days when you can't accept your part,
Days where you tremble down
Like a leaf from an autumn alarm.
It's okay. Even the moon disappears
When shine becomes for granted,
Or when no one cares
For the poetry of moon being unwanted.
Even the moon contains flaws-
Of being dark and patchy of lovers' odds.
How come you be the best of the best,
When nature can't make
The light of dark to be the best?
Cherish the flaws you contain,
Like when love become blind,

When heart sings serene.
Accept the days when your incapabilities
Become the light of the lime-
When gym can't rush adrenaline,
Or when maths can't become an answer friend,
When rejection drives from flaws within,
Or when lack of motivation
Can't lift you again.
Sit, speculate and stand again.
You have me being you-
To cherish your stand again...

3. Over-Giving

Why do I do over?
Over-care, or
Over-concern?
Don't you think your *over* is someone's limit?
Your care is someone's irritation,
Your concern is someone's frustration.
I know you have it all to give,
Because at times you missed it-
Your heart wanted the similar pampering,
But the carousel had some different liking.
The ride went way too fast
To give it all back to you.
Your pockets went empty,
With nothing left for you.
The word over in itself is a limit complete-
How could you expect
Care more than a limit complete?
Don't do that *over*,
Because it's not meant for them.
Your care and concern

Are way too much for them.
Your intentions and emotions
Are too pure to be divine-
How could a sinful man grasp all fine?
They do take you for granted,
And for them, you don't matter.
Your purity is a stain
On their divine dishonouring terrain.
Preserve your love,
The concerns you have,
As very few men alive on earth have.
Maybe later they realise
What did they lose-
From the boundless love
To the one caring ado.
It's you-
From mirage to reality,
From concern to clarity.
What all you have
Is first meant for you.
Cherish it, live it,
And then distribute!

4. The Tyranny of Stares

The statues of spy that stand tall at lanes,
Their pendulum tongue spitting drains.
Their haunted eyes that nothing hides-
From venomous plight to judgmental stripe.
Their whisper chisels your name,
Their stare examines your action game.
From movement to thoughts,
From body and mind across.
From the ones I meet,
Or the way I greet,
For what others wear,
Or what they choose as theirs-
These eyes are terror.
They sip assumptions like vintage red wine,
And serve the gossips as glamour divine.
Don't worry, as this eve they dine;
At an eve, they'll be *the* dine.
For the stars still burn, though the night may be cruel—
And truth needs no jury, no scorn, and no rule.

5. The Monster And Me

There lies a monster inside me
That eats me out like a blueberry pie-
A monster that fears my heart,
Like darkness eating enlightened spy.

I doubt whether I'm enough or not.
I doubt whether they like it or not.
I doubt if I will suffice as a friend-
The one trustworthy and emotionally bent.

I doubt if I'm okay to be not okay again.
I doubt whether my sadness is fine,
Or my anger has to be well defined.
I doubt I should clarify my need or not,
Or just remain silent like nothing happened at all.

I think I am doing *over*, or what?
Or is the front one just ignoring it all?
I doubt whether my incompleteness is fine.
I think- for whom my existence is well-defined?

I fear whether my sadness would grasp it all.
Would they leave because I'm not worthy at all?
Am I just full to be half again,
Or so half to not get full again?

Am I someone they'll like or not-
A member of their good book, or just a person abroad?
Should I just act good to be good to them,
Or should I say yes to their every questionable bent?

Is it too needy to say yes always,
Or too creepy to be sad always?
I oscillate between this *may* or *may not,*
Like the monster eating in between every halt.

I doubt if I fall in between-
Will they accept me or leave me in between?
How much good or how much bad?
It's nothing yours; it's nothing mad.

You lose yourself in battle for others.
You win with them against yourself.
You try not to be sad again-
Hiding tears or pain again-
But for them, it doesn't matter that much,
Against their will of themselves.

How much cool or how much hot?
Am I not enough to be at all?
Why to be full if half is fine?
Your sadness, anger-need not to be defined.

It's *you* the way you see yourself,
From eyes of yours, from view of yourself.
The mirror casts the image of you-
From silence to scream, to trauma to be *you.*

Everything is *you,* like you want to be.
What will they do if you are not your own to be?
For whom you want to be so good-
Were they like you when you thought they would?

It's not to reciprocate to be bad for bad,
It's just-don't be bad because others are bad.
Don't be bad. Don't have a doubt.
Your existence does have an inevitable shout-out.

From every phase to every dilemma,
You need to be yours-against all odds.
No monster will eat, no terror shall fear.
If you're yourself, then you'll care.

Care your heart, your sadness,

Your happiness apart,
Care your mind, your fall,
Or your journey apart.

Care yourself, care your need.
You stand tall against every flee.

6. The Battle Within

Recall those nights
When the heart became impatient
To be patient of attack-
An attack from the vestiges of past,
From the memoir of people,
Or the actions of self.

When the world started trembling
Like the leaves during a heavy blow,
The world converged in eyes
Like entering in a black hole.

How harsh it was to be unknown
Of what's happening known.
From the shattering heart
To the drowning mind-
Everything was a havoc
Until it all became mine.

Every night when the mind speaks

Of what I did now or then,
Of what others did now or then,
Of what happened or thought would happen-
The rotting self or the peaceful self-
I found bliss in mayhem hell.

How to control the heart's eagerness
To accept or not this mental health?
Whether it's ruining the life, or
Giving a soothing plight-
Where pain becomes friend
And everything seems alright.

Listen, my dear,
Your heart now weighs way too heavy-
From the shackles of liveliness
To the agony and worldly fury.

Cry out loud and be yourself.
Don't take pills and be your help.
Share yourself to the one outcoming;
Be fearless of what he or she will think.

Journal yourself or talk to yourself-
You aren't mad or unhealthy.
You are just way too *you*
To be healthy and wonderful,

Like the bliss of the Almighty,
Like the light of the golden hour.
My dear,
Just have some mercy.

7. The Unseen Fears

Fear, a four-letter word
Carrying weight of a thousand tons on the heart.
Fear, a simple word
Having depth deeper than fathoms apart.
Fear, a word frightening terror.
Fear, a word escaping zones withered.

We all have some fear-
A fear of failure, a fear of unable to meet near,
Fear of being unfriended,
Fear of unable to be chosen,
Fear of being left behind.
Fear of being a boring nerd behind,
Fear of being lonely in a group,
Or like left alone to decide whether *you being choose*.

Your heart is perplexed
From the insecurity of life and its people.
Your mind is vague
From the agony of traitors.

You fear to be clear and honest.
You fear to be sad and plutonic.
You fear your past to get define.
You fear your present to be left undermined.
You fear your future to be left behind-
Like the forgotten pages of books unmined.

The pain is real.
The dilemma is true.
How have you been here is simply beautiful.
How much the stars scream against moon,
But left secondary when love blooms.
I hate you being true
From miles away or a few metres to flee.

8. The Social Battery

How strange it becomes
When people around you start haunting
Like the house of dead's,
Where there's no courage
To be themselves.

When fear indebts in the
Surrounding of beings,
The heart feel insecurity
And the fear of being demeaned.

Where there lies
No beauty of togetherness,
Rather aura full of loneliness.

When the social battery
Of being unwantedly included
Goes negatively down,
When heart drowns
And, the brain doesn't rebound.

When the cycle of interaction
Feels like a pressure
Of being talkative and amiable
To people with no regards together.

When words seem to lose charm,
And the laughter is a mere demand.
When agreement is a way avoidant
Just to avoid the mere respondent.

How cruel it becomes
To sit, speak and spark,
When brain rots and leaves no spark.

I know, this pressure
Of acting happily involved,
When you yourself feel uninvolved.

When what you feel
Feels like a burden of debt-
Just know, you are your battery.
You have your charger.
Give yourself the time to charge
With clear boundaries and set remarks.

As that's what life is-

To live, charge, and come back.
The mantra of happiness
And the art of smiling-
Maybe it becomes too hectic to ask,
Or too lonely to combat.

Just know, it's you and it's yours.
Give acceptance to happiness,
Even in the abode dark.
As sometimes darkness too
Bring light enough
To be yours and happily yours!

9. Quietly Conflicted

In the arcade of time, the same scare did come back;
The scars and the vestiges jolted for a wrath,
I call it mine, without being mine.
Frightened child again cried!

He thought he overpowered the fear of people.
Yes, an unheard anxiety of people and people;
An unheard anxiety of haunting time unreal,
An anxiety that drives away from people to people,
An anxiety that crosses talks and gossips, for real.

The time when words seem to vanish,
The time when thoughts appear misty,
The time when face pale to sicky,
The time when the heart aches serenity.

What is this serenity?
Why is willing want to be unwanted?
Why does light in eyes appear dimming,
Or laughter of people hauntingly screaming?

Why does the minuscule time seem a day long?
I don't know what exactly the heart wants?

Sometimes it wants to be surrounded by people;
Or sometimes just aloof crying for real.
Sometimes a glimmer of stare seems haunting,
Words lose charm and heart cries shouting.

In instances I don't want anyone,
The other I cry for no one.
What is this state of an unwanted want?
Why is this anxious thought so wan?

In tears often I shed my disorder,
By not speaking I share my shudder.
Neither I speak nor I share,
I don't know what state you call it for real?

Am I feeling things so much,
Or I'm being emotionless,
Am I expecting too much
Or just flowing from things away?

I certainly think being quiet is alright.
I don't know why I think, is alright right?
I believe time takes time for timeless things,
Till then try not to be quiet!

10. The Survivor's Anthem

The world acts too tough
For a fragile heart doing too much.
The world and its people
Are stupid enough
To not regard the hard worth.

I know, how tough it is
To not get what you desired
Or maybe what you deserved.
Like the crusaders fighting battle,
Or the one just living to be better.

How patience and hard work it needs
To be consistent proving yourself,
Or to be the one acting enough
Just to make the heart feel the self.

I know,
The dedication, the hard work you did,
The effervescent efforts and the nights you lived,

The tears that rolled and the pain that supports,
The world that slept when your eyes swelled.
The heart that needed time,
The body wanted redefine,
The face that structured away,
Or the time that swept away.
When you lose your friends' fun,
Or your favourites return,
When the dilemma of sufficiency questioned,
Of how you did was left hidden.
When no one knows the trauma
The heart and body held
To shine out as victors of vying
Or the brittle hands to lift the achievement sublime.

Always remember, you are seen,
You are heard.
The stories that no one knows
Pens on the chambers and valves of love.

The tears, the eyes, the body, the face,
The trophies, the marks, the tortured gaze,
The silence, the trauma, the efforts you did
Are all acknowledged and appraised.

But you question the presence of appraisal
From others the way you wanted,

Gives disappointment and sadness planted.

Always know, you are the survivor
Of all that you underwent-
From every night to time that went.
Go and treat yourself,
Listen to music that sooths yourself,
Have delicacies from Chinese to continental,
From waffle to drinks to brownie-mental.

That's your acceptance to what you went.
Now you are known,
Now you are heard,
From all the efforts and stories unsent!

11. You Are Not Apart

I know how things become
Heavy for you to manage.
How people don't treat you
The way you wanted.
I know how sad your heart feels
When no one encounters your silence.
I know when you push yourself
To engage with others.
When your presence or absence
Doesn't even matter to others.

I know when the circle
Becomes different for you.
When a table full of people
Seem empty to you.
Even a room filled with people
Doesn't provide the warmth together.
Maybe a sudden silence
Breaks the sadness further.

How you feel is completely fine.
They treat you wrong
Must not be undermined.

Remember, you have you with you
When the silence quiets,
It's you who screams
At the epitome of your voice.
When you shout and scream accompany,
You get the lonely symphony.

From the odds of you
To the odds of others,
Accept you out of others.
Don't be cruel to yourself.

Be the light of the dark.

When the days are hard,
Smile and go ahead.
Because you are not apart.

12. The Own Woven Mess

Understanding me is a task abound,
From one to another rebound.
Not a thought of a single edge,
But a tangible woven mess.

Unlike the disparity of heart and mind,
I stand doubtful on my own side.
What I need or what I didn't,
Hopelessly hopeful for tasks many.
Craving for loneliness, I hate being lonely,
Fearful heart still thinks of the impossible ends.
An agathokakological me,
Finding something logical in me.
Hatred for others on tongue,
With utmost concern in heart.
How am I or who am I, who knows?
It is hard to accept such me,
It is hard to convey such me,
It is hard to understand such me,
No one is actually there for me.

From stories to poems alone,
From happiness to sadness soon.
I hate being sad but love sadness.
Who knows who am I?
Does anyone need me,
Or I am just a burden undefined?

What friendship what relations
I am not good for people for being so me.
Being me hates me sometimes,
But being me is what I have in me.

Who understands, who cares?
It's me who's left against everyone.
Why it's me, or what for me?
Who is for me, why for me?

Maybe I'm not easy to love,
But I'm still learning, still enough.
In this quiet war I fight,
I might just find my own light.

13. Ink, Tears and Love

From the shackles of memories,
The heart writes the story of love.
From the ink drenching tears,
The heart writes the poetry unheard.
From the shells of pains
And the well serene,
The heart screams the name of the beloved.

The tears rolling down,
The shady curse of loneliness-
The heart forbids the acceptance of dearth
And the lover's emptiness.

From days passing by unwantedly,
The heart craves the lover's call.
From missing texts to no missed calls,
The heart dwells into eternal fall.

From the fall of misery
To the grave glittery,

Writes the name of you-
The name unheard, unspoken and unknown,
And the name to everyone's known!
Yes, it's you-
I love you!

14. The Garden of Love

The boy asks the girl,
"Why do you write love as dead roses?"

And she speaks:
"You love me like dead roses-
That lasts eternal,
Smells ethereal,
And feels ephemeral.
You live as bookmarks
Between the pages of my book-
That worth revisiting.
You live in between the columns of my diary
As a scent of love and memory.
Your presence garlands the pages,
Your scent reminisces about the glazes."

Amusingly perplexed he asked:
"Let the love feel alive-
Why a rotten, love define?
A living rose is loved for its beauty-

From the drenching drop,
Like the lips slippery,
And the fresh scent as petrichor.
How could it be so dull across?"

Further she claims
"A rose alive is loved for her beauty,
But the dead one is beyond beauty.
A living rose contains the scent,
But the dead one has memory descent.
A living rose lives for life,
But the dead one beyond afterlife."

With a sign of blush, he says
"For me, I love you as a garden full of roses-
Sunflowers, daisies, marigolds, orchids and tulips.
I'll keep the rotten petals as your eternal love.
I'll cherish the beauty as serenity- the god does.
I'll not just care, but love your every part-
The bright petals to the pale ones,
The rising high or the dull, dead ones-
The phase from scent to heart's descent.
For me, loving you is all I do."

She smiles and thinks:
"He raised the flowers
Which made me feel alive.

The one I love or hate by.
He loves me, he loves my part
How to say that loving him is my only task!"

15. A Silent Table

A silent table
Holds words more than a filled one.
Where words fail, thoughts broken,
And minds separated,
The heart calls for some sensation-
A sensation that could move the table ahead,
From silence to motion,
With words and gossips ahead.

Who says people make the table empty?
The table full of people
Seems emptier than a lonely one-
The one that hold people but cannot glue them,
The one that speaks to me but not to them,
The one that has everyone but shares no one.
A silent table
Holds words more than a filled one.

16. When Time Isn't Enough

Giving time is definitely self-healing,
But how could giving time heal the other?

For a person who rush with thoughts-
From future to past across,
Thinking for all possible present,
The future outburst, or maybe the distance.
The fearing awkwardness shedding sweat,
The shut mouth, the deadly stare,
The crushing intensity to hear the other,
The crushing intensity to say further.
The time unbridging the two together,
The crawling crab to come together.

How it could all vanish from time immemorial?
How time can heal the unsaid wounds' burial?

I can definitely give time-
But not more than a limit.
Come to me, with all your grudges;

I'll accept our parts, explain my heart,
Apologise for every part.
Because for me, you matter-
And time keeps us apart!

17. I Promise

I promise
I'd stop writing about you from tomorrow.
Every morrow,
I wait for you to come back-
But
I don't expect you to come back.

How ironic things have been,
How drastic we have been-
From promises of every morrow
To empty days tomorrow.

As you said that
It's too harsh to be together,
And too close to be away,
Days have been so *too...*
To be penned away.

I promise
Today I'll write you to the final-

I forgot,
It's tomorrow!

18. The Awkward Journey

I embark on a journey awkward
From people unbothered
To the memory altered.

From lanes full of silences
To hearts screaming aloud-
Why suddenly so awkward?
Why people so unbothered?
Why hearts seem screaming
While the mouth shut speaking?
Why the faces act crafty
While the gestures different partly?
How humans juxtapose their feelings,
How cruel they act so lovingly-
To garland others with comfort and bliss,
They erode their rose field with pain and hits.

In haste of comfort, they forget cure,
In haste of procure, they lose the pure!

19. Seventeen Days And Still

It's been seventeen days since you left.
I hope this finds you when you miss me ahead.

Days have gone in a shallow darkness-
Something is missing in every aspect.
It feels I've lost a person in a person,
The one I reached every now and then,
The one I claimed was "my serene,"
The one who brought the child out of me,
Like the flowers blooming in sprouting spring.
The one who sort the worrisome me,
Like healing becomes easier for me.
You had been close; you had been me-
I've not lost you but someone *me.*

I'll not claim my happiness bygone,
I'd rather cherish the one stronger rebound.
My happiness lies in the essence of you.
As a lover, you lived in the heart of mine-

Now you live in memories benign.

How could I forget you from the marvellous time?
From lanes to malls to the dancing drops divine-
The season changed from unshackled to shackled,
The distance equates to the love of mine.

If missing you gave me extra breaths,
Then the god have been so jealous of you,
O divine!
You're the cruel cure of my heart-
A body where a withered heart lives happily apart.

20. The Room That Knows Me

A room holds a lot of memories
From the laughter of children
To the darkest of memory.

The walls of the room are victims
Of the most human catastrophe.

With pain striking every corner
And tears lining the whole length.
With posters screaming on every wall.
To the lonely roof that lends-
The nights alone with darkest of the hours,
The days oblong with time so difficult to par.
The windows wide open
For fresh breeze to entangle with hairs,
The panics brushes
When the bliss connects.

This room owns and brought up me,

Knows things more than me.
How could I stay aloof?
How could I be lonesome,
When everything is here so wholesome?

The room that explores the many shades of mine,
Explaining the definition of silence that undermines.

21. I Hope When Death Comes To Me

I hope when death comes to me,
It finds me alive to mortal me.

I hope when death comes to me,
It finds me pale to engross me.

I hope when death comes to me,
It finds me in the gloomy happiness.

I hope when death comes to me,
It finds me loving to accept destiny.

I hope when death comes to me,
It sees the unhealed wounds to carry.

I hope when death comes to me,
It wipes the tears that freezes on me.

I hope when death comes to me,

It finds me glaring at the dead divine.
I hope when death comes to me,
It finds me singing the carols of my life.

I hope when death comes to me,
When death remains undefined.

My eyes aren't misty,
For something incomplete left behind.

I hope death comes to me,
I want death to come to me!

22. I Want To Cry

I want to cry the depth loud my voice,
Even when the voice cracks,
Or the heart misses its one beat,
Even when the scars come up,
Or the world starts to freeze.
Even when the hands shimmer,
Or the world seems incomplete.
Even if there's no one to see,
I want to cry the depth loud my voice.

I want to cry the depth down my heart,
Even when the heart collapse,
Or the drowned sorrow rises apart.
Even if the memory loses its trauma,
Or the pain shows the dram,
Even when the beat hastens its speed,
Or the running blood feels incomplete.
Even when the brain starts to speak,
Or the heart transcends humanity,
I want to cry the depth down my heart.

I want to cry but want a shoulder to lean,
I want to cry but need someone by me.
I want to cry with someone holding my hand,
I want to cry with someone entangling my headbands.
I want to cry with my head on someone's lap,
I want to cry with someone saying-
"I'm there, just cry!"
I want to cry but just can't cry,
As no one knows how to make someone cry!

23. Perplexed

I feel perplexed-
When I write love,
Whole out of my heart.
And pain,
Whole out of my heart.
But sees-
Both standing similar,
On same ends apart.

24. Florist's Madness

I've loved pain
Since the very start.
For me, it's not a nuisance,
Rather an element of life apart.

I love people with happiness,
As they stand differ with me.
They show me truth
Against the dim mist.
Since my life started
They sow a sunflower alone,
Against the blooming heat of sun.
It dies all alone, leaving no turn.
I need a pair to stand and live,
Against the scorching brightness.
I need affection, love even as a dead,
To fruit again like florist's madness!

25. I Will Come To You Mate When...

I will come to you mate,
When your absence doesn't itch me hard.

I will come to you mate,
When your presence isn't all my part.

I will come to you mate,
When things surround, stop hurting heart.

I will come to you mate,
When your ignorance doesn't hurt me hard.

I will come to you mate,
When I rejoice, your absence apart.

I will come to you mate,
When silent mouth isn't awkward apart.

I will come to you mate,

When nothing makes me feel apart.

I will come to you mate,
When I accept being the other part.

I will come to you mate,
When sadness isn't my hazard.

I will come to you mate,
When all I have is me at last.

I will come to you mate,
When I feel fine in an empty room.

I will come to you mate,
When you aren't there for me in cocoon.

I will come to you mate,
When life teaches me to love my heart.

I will come to you mate,
When I keep myself over your part.

I will come to you mate,
When your actions don't define my art.

I will come to you mate,

When I don't need your supporting part.

I will come to you mate,
When I stop begging your company apart.

I will come to you mate,
When your behavior doesn't doubt my part.

I will come to you mate,
When I need myself to treat my heart.

I will come to you mate,
When all I have is me at last!

26. You Are Your Divine

Unstitch the stiches on the mouth,
Relieve the worldly burden
From mind's mount.

Dance in the rain despite the gloomy serene,
With fearless shadow under contemplation,
The frightened heart in deep meditation.

The eyes rolling the tears of relief-
You need healing
From the world and your own belief.

From scars and wounds to untreated gloom,
Like joining the broken pottery in Kintsugi,
Or mending heart's own tapestry.
Like Prometheus unchained
From the force of love-
Don't ache the bent back
Against the tall will of being fine.

Take time and heal yourself
Because you are your divine!

www.ingramcontent.com/pod-product-compliance
Lightning Source LLC
La Vergne TN
LVHW021241200726
843509LV00012B/1559